IS ALWAYS
BOASTFUL
AND NEVE
NOT TAKI
LOVE DO
FINDS ITS
TO MAKE ALLOWANCES, TO TRUST, TO HOPE AND
TO ENDURE WHATEVER COMES.

Welcome to this little book of meditations, prayers and activities about Love, inspired by the verses in the book of Corinthians.

In Paul's first letter to the Christians of Corinth in Greece he spends a long time instructing, advising, challenging and encouraging the young church there. He hasn't visited for a few years and he knows of the immorality in the wealthy pagan city and the divisions that have emerged within the church. Although he aims to not diminish the message of the cross with 'wisdom and eloquence' he gave us some of the most powerful and well-known verses of the New Testament.

Chapter thirteen contains some of them.

It is probably the most popular Bible passage chosen to be read at weddings, the words are read to remind the happy couple what the foundation of marriage should be, and the congregation what the foundation of life itself should be. The words tell us that love is at the root of living in community with each other and in harmony with God.

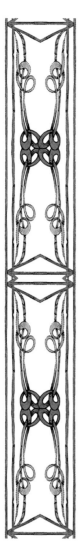

It will be the only thing that will remain when everything else has gone.

Whilst having many meanings, the word love is used in the Bible with great power,

> Jesus said, "A new command I give you: Love one another. As I have loved you, so you must love one another."
>
> and
>
> "For God so loved the world that he gave His one and only Son, that whoever believes in Him shall not perish but have eternal life."

The kind of love Jesus spoke about was completely unconditional, self-sacrificing and pure. Many people today use the word 'love' with the same kind of disregard as they cry out to God when they really want to say "Wow isn't that amazing / awful / shocking / gorgeous!".

If we could communicate the power of love (without using cheesy pop songs) we could share the mind-blowing possibilities of a world where love is the first thought and the first action.

Please look at the comments at the back of this book for some additional thoughts and ideas.

With every blessing,

Mary & Mark Fleeson
Holy Island

love IS
patient

You've probably heard the phrases 'patience is a virtue', 'good things come to those who wait' and Teresa of Avila's 'Patient endurance attaineth to all things.' But have you ever thought about the true meaning of patience?

The dictionary definition is: 'The capacity to accept or tolerate delay, problems, or suffering without becoming annoyed or anxious.'

That's a massive challenge Paul is encouraging us to meet. First he reminds us of Jesus' commandment to love one another (John 13:34) then he tells us just what love is and is not. His challenge is that we express our love for others in a very real way, by the example of the way we live and by the way we interact with others. Realistically we know that we will get both annoyed and anxious, life's just like that, but we don't have to bear the burdens that cause those worries, alone.

Try listing your anxieties and annoyances on a piece of paper, cut or tear each one out and lay them on the cross on the next page. As you do so deliberately hand them to God. (You could colour the cross too.)

'Come to me, all you who are weary and burdened, and I will give you rest.
Matt.11:28

IS
kind

How many words mean the same as 'kind'?
Just some of them are listed below. Add them
into the mix of what love is and consider
how easy or difficult it is to add them
to your daily life.

AFFECTIONATE
AMIABLE
CHARITABLE
COMPASSIONATE
CONSIDERATE
KINDHEARTED
SYMPATHETIC
THOUGHTFUL
CORDIAL
COURTEOUS
FRIENDLY
GENTLE
GRACIOUS
HUMANE
TOLERANT
KINDLY
LOVING

As you think about each of the
words that mean 'kind' shade in
a line of the figure.

IS

not boastful

The dashing hero of a nineteenth century novel may have a 'proud and noble bearing' but in real relationships pride, if the word is used to mean excessive self-esteem and boasting about ones qualities and achievements, can only bring trouble.

Many of us grew up with the wise sayings of the Book of Proverbs, including the one that reminds us of pride coming before a fall but perhaps that isn't what we need to hear today when we can all think of prideful people who have got on in life apparently very well. Perhaps we need to hear that appearances can be deceptive, and the struggle to appear to have everything 'sorted' leaves no time or energy for anyone else.

In contrast vulnerability, the conscious choice to reveal your true self, gives those around you permission to do the same and in that freedom relationships can flourish. Love is being yourself, with all your weaknesses and flaws on show, not to gain sympathy or concessions but to be truly real.

PRIDE COMES BEFORE DISASTER, AND ARROGANCE BEFORE A FALL. BETTER TO BE HUMBLE WITH THE NEEDY THAN TO DIVIDE PLUNDER WITH THE PROUD.

PROVERBS 16:18-19

Love is not conceited

ot on the heels of pride comes conceit and both words are
nked by the word arrogance. The opposite word is humility,
ve is humility and yet to be humble has many negative
nnotations in todays society. It means to be modest, shy, meek,
wly, abased, passive, timid, submissive, docile, bashful...I'm not
ntirely sure I want to be defined as all of those things,
y feminist, educated, Western ego screams out in protestation
t the thought that to express love I have to be abased or timid,
t alone docile or bashful!

nd yet in the presence of God we can shed the ego and safely
t go of all the masks of ego, even the definitions become
eaningless. Without the trappings of conceit we are raw
umans, vulnerable and exposed like newborns.
hen we die to self we are truly born again. (Galatians 2:20)

LOVE IS never rude

We all want to be rude at times, shout from our car at the tailgater or the driver who cuts us up on the roundabout, then there's the people who queue jump and the ones who let the door slam in your face...then there's those who have no respect for people or property... But to approach life with an attitude of love is to very deliberately put others before yourself and to treat them as you would like to be treated.

Our aim then, is not to always be polite or clean or sophisticated or frail, all literal opposites of 'rude', but instead to be Christ-like in all we do. Think about how our response to others can affect them by using the example at the side.

Fred woke up with a headache so he snapped at his wife, Sara, for no reason.

Sara started to worry about Fred and their marriage and she left the house late, when she got to work she was reprimanded and in her frustration she gave her assistant extra work.

Her assistant missed her Mother's birthday dinner because she had to work late.

Her Mum was so upset that she shouted at her husband on the way home.

He lost his concentration due to the row and didn't see the cat in the road.

The owner of the cat *dot dot dot*

Obviously that is a very simplistic and unlikely scenario but try to imagine how it could have been different if each person had responded in a Christ-like manner.

LOVE never seeks its own advantage

The message of treating others as you would like to be treated (Luke 6:31) is re-enforced by Love being defined as not being 'self-seeking' or 'selfish'.

LOVE IS PUTTING OTHERS FIRST

LOVE does not take offence

It's easy to be offended by all sorts of things, and how much offence we take can depend on our mood and energy levels. Some days we will just feel 'got at' and even innocent remarks will seem laden with insult.

At times like that we need a cure, a soothing, perfect balm to heal the situation before it becomes unmanageable...

P
E
R **PRAY** for the person and the situation
F
E **FORGIVE** the person and yourself.
C
T **B**LESS the person.
A
L
MOVE ON, don't over think it.

does not store up grievances

Bearing a grudge is never going to be a good choice in life, it doesn't solve anything and the only thing it changes is the person holding on to it, it eats away at the spirit and the mind until it becomes a great big, unmanageable ball of resentment and pain.

If there is any grievance you are holding onto -
Let it go.
Now.
It's not an option to keep it.
It cannot exist alongside love.

Use the prayer below and the image over the page to help you.

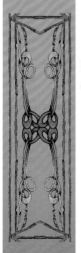

Help me to forgive
Help me to forgive myself
Help me to love
Help me to desire love in my life
more than to want to hold on to resentment
Bring healing into the situation
Bring healing into my life

Imagine each ball is a resentment that you've been holding. Imagine that as you forgive it becomes impossible to hold. Imagine dropping it into the deepest sea. If the bitter memories return repeat the process. You could use real pebbles and throw them into deep water.

does not rejoice in wrong doing

Or...

Don't be entertained by unrighteous actions! That can mean many things, from laughing at someone telling offensive jokes to feeling smug that someone you don't like has lost their job. Most of you reading this probably wouldn't do those things but every day we are fed lies about people, places and life in general. We are drip fed a false view of the world either to make us consume the 'solutions' or to hide the stark truths so that we don't despair. The truth of any situation can be hard to find so God offers us the gift of discernment (1 Cor. 12:10), the ability to hear God's guidance and distinguish between good and evil beyond the obvious evidence, where the lines are blurry and even hidden. Ask for that gift if you are not aware that you have it.

Rejoice when you experience good, rejoice when you meet love in action and rejoice in the exposure of truth.

IS **finding joy in truth**

love IS making allowances

Make allowance for each other's faults, and forgive anyone who offends you. Remember, the Lord forgave you, so you must forgive others. Col. 3:13

Always be humble and gentle. Be patient with each other, making allowance for each other's faults because of your love. Eph. 4:2

Is it easier to make allowances for those whom you know? Those who perhaps you have some empathy for or understanding of? Do we subconsciously make decisions about how much we will forgive someone's behaviour? Of course we do! If we read about someone breaking the law we make assumptions about that person, if we hear about a person having an affair then we will probably try to guess at the personalities of those involved. It is such a common habit to judge others that we can forget how far it deviates from Jesus' teaching.

When the Jewish leaders brought an adulterous woman to Jesus for him to comment on her punishment (stoning was the Law passed down from Moses), he said "Let any one of you who is without sin be the first to throw a stone at her." Jesus would not condemn the woman and none of the others present could truly say they themselves were innocent.

The challenge to us is to resist the habit of judging others and to accept them as they are, even if they judge and reject us.

Love is ready to trust

One of the hardest things to do is to trust in others or in things or situations. Although as children we have a trusting nature, logic and experience tells us that humans are fallible and will let us down; things are ephemeral and will decay; and situations can change in the blink of an eye. But despite the teachings of the world around us God wants us to experience that child-like trust as adults.

One expression of trust is to pray. In prayer we expose our deeper self in vulnerability and hope, we are not passively asking a distant entity to answer our requests. We are, with the inspiration of the Holy Spirit, actively campaigning for God's will to be done in our lives and the lives of others. And we are trusting that God hears our plea.

LET OUR VOICES RISE LIKE INCENSE
LET THEM BE AS SWEET PERFUME
LET OUR PRAISES FILL THE TEMPLE
HALLELUJAH'S RINGING EVER NEW
HOLY HOLY IS THE LORD ALMIGHTY, HOLY HOLY IS THE LORD OUR GO
LINDA BELL WHITME

love is ready to hope

AND GOD WILL WIPE AWAY EVERY TEAR FROM THEIR EYES; THERE SHALL BE NO MORE DEATH, NOR SORROW, NOR CRYING. THERE SHALL BE NO MORE PAIN, FOR THE FORMER THINGS HAVE PASSED AWAY." REVELATION 21:4

LOVE IS

ready to endure

to hold out against; sustain without impairment or yielding; undergo; to bear without resistance or with patience; tolerate; brave; encounter; experience; face; feel; go through; know; ride out; suffer; sustain; tolerate; undergo; weather; withstand.

Try to imagine what the world might be like if everyone showed love in the ways described in Corinthians, and showed that love every day of their lives. We would live in a world transformed. Practising these ways of loving can transform individual lives.
Be a part of changing the world.

And now these three remain: faith, hope and love.

But the greatest of these is love.

Comments and Encouragements

Take time out. Just ten minutes a day or half an hour twice a week set aside purely for being in God's presence can make a big difference to how your spiritual life grows. Find a quiet place and give the time you have to God, you could use the following prayer:

> This day, O God is Yours, May it be good, May it be right,
> May it be filled with Your presence.

Pray like it's as vital as breathing. Sometimes we place praying, like God, into box. We think God can only be met or talked to in Church or when a certa person is present, in reality we were created to communicate with our Creator, to enjoy a two-way conversation which never ends. There's so mu God wants to share with us, to show us and teach us, so pray constantly a be aware of Gods presence in all things.

Look for God in the small things. The snatched conversation you just had with the shop assistant, God was there; the hug you gave your grieving friend, God was there; the moment you took to smell the flowers, God was there; when you washed up after dinner, God was there. It isn't that God wants t do the washing up for you or promise you that every washing up moment will be filled with joy but God may be telling you that if you spend those times that need little thought, in prayer and conversation with your Creator, then your life may be that bit richer and purposeful.

I should point out that if you don't pray during the washing up your life will not fall apart, I know that sometimes I'm so tired that I can't even form a coherent thought let alone pray sensibly and a few minutes of mindless washing up is a pleasurable chance to switch off. If you can't pray then try singing or humming and just be open to whatever God may want to say to you.

Never 'beat yourself up' for not doing enough, practice just being and be available when God calls you to do something.

Allow yourself to be vulnerable to others and to God. It's not easy to do but when we allow others to see our true selves they will see more of God and God will be able to use you more effectively to help others.